THE SKY INSIDE YOUR BODY

THE SKY INSIDE YOUR BODY

Poets of Queens Press
Yara Arts Group
New York, 2022

Photograph of author by Alexandr Khantaev.
Book front and back covers by Waldemart Klyuzko.
Designed and composed by Oleksandr Fraze-Frazenko.

Copyright © 2022 Christina Turczyn. All rights reserved. Printed in The USA. No part of this work may be reproduced or used in any form by any means — graphic, electronic or mechanical, including photocopying, recording, taping or usage in information storage and retrieval systems — without prior written permission of the authors, except for brief extracts for the purpose of review of this book.

ISBN 978-1-7351478-7-1

CONTENTS

At the Level of Bone 12
Witness 13
After 9/11 14
That Year 15
Leaving Harvard 16
Your Laughter, Running 18
Zhuravli 19
You Are 20
Social Distancing 21
Chance 25
A Daughter's Song 26
There Should Be 28
Accident 29
Other 31
Lena speaks: 32
You Tell Me 33
Van Gogh: Church at Auvers-sur-Oise 34
Winter Morning, Montclair 35
Past the half-life 36
Tattoos 37

X-Ray of a Winter Landscape 40
X-Ray of a Winter Landscape 41
Matryoshka 45
Thinking 47
A Practical Poetics 48
In the Camp 50
What Words? 51
Dream's Long River 52
The Violence of Things Unnoticed 54
Fractals of Rain 55

The Sky Inside Your Body 58
I Walked 59
Freshman Composition 61
Untitled 63
In Search of Stories 64
Let Me Be You 65
I Could Have Told You 67
Ask Yourself 68
Ulster Heights, New York 70
Elsewhere 72
Winter Coat 73

With Doors Wide Open 74
Gravity 75
Clay Birds 76
Renaming 77
Cobalt 78
At School 79
I Don't Remember 81
Maps Carved on Stone 82
With Doors Wide Open 83

Acknowledgements:

With complete gratitude to the members of the Yara Arts Group, a resident company at the La MaMa Experimental Theatre, especially to Olena Jennings and Virlana Tkacz, whose unwavering support of my work throughout the years can only be described as miraculous.

With great appreciation to former publishers Phillip Levine, Laurence Carr, and Maria Mazziotti Gillan.

My thanks, also, to the publications in which these poems first appeared:

Apiary Blog ("Accident").

Art Times Journal ("Dream's Long River," "Van Gogh: Church at Auvers-sur-Oise").

Chronogram ("At Home," "Tattoos,""There Should Be," "The Violence of Things Unnoticed," "Witness," "Winter Morning, Montclair").

Chickaree Press. "Fractals of Rain," "Past the Half-Life of Grief" *(Lifeblood: Woodstock Poetry Society).*

Codhill Press ("Untitled," and "Ulster Heights, N.Y.") *Riverine: An Anthology of Hudson Valley Writers.*

Exposed Literary Magazine ("Song of the Cranes," "Let Me Be You").

Gulfstreaming ("Ask Yourself," "What Words," "You Tell Me).

Lightwood —Life and the Arts in the 21st Century ("Social Distancing").

Mohonk Mountain Stage Company. ("I Could Have Told You"*).*

The Paterson Literary Review ("Freshman Composition," "Leaving Harvard," "A Practical Poetics").

The Poetry Center, Passaic County Community College (Celebrating William Carlos Williams and the Poetry of Place: North Jersey in Poetry ("I Walked").

Ukrainian American Poets Respond ("Elsewhere," "Winter Coat").

The Woodstock Poetry Society ("Lena Speaks").

The following organizations are thanked for their awards:

Global Commitment Foundation Poetry Award, for the performance piece, "A Place without Statues," rendered at the Re-Imagine Ourselves Arts Festival, Yara Arts Group, 2012.

Associated Writing Programs: Intro Award in Poetry, 1994.

Cutthroat, a Journal of the Arts. Joy Harjo Poetry Competition Finalist. 2007.

Mohonk Mountain Stage Company. Vanguard Voices of the Hudson Valley. Awarded first prize and honorable mention, 2007.

Salem College Center for Women Writers: Rita Dove National Poetry Awards, Honorable Mention, 2004

The Paterson Poetry Center, for the Allen Ginsberg Poetry Award (First Prize) 1999; Honorable Mention, 1992.

At the Level of Bone

Witness

My grandmother gathered
bread for sparrows.
At the end of the week, she scattered
dry crumbs in the yard.

Was she waiting for something unnamed to return?
A brother, a prisoner, a storm?
Some shy angel, freed from duty at the bar?

Or was this the road home—
Word after word thrown out to the cold,
bones laid bare
for witness?

After 9/11

What is the shape of air
around a man's stooped shoulders?
Is it that of a low-flying swallow,
a woman breathing in, a tree of cloud?
Those of us who are afraid of traveling,
watch poems re-enter our mouths.
The moon of the heart never rises,
even on the clearest of nights.

You and I, degrees of light
darkening on water. Tell me where
the body ends, and suffering begins.
Does the body end with words?
Does it begin with night air pressing
against the brittle salt of living, and finish
with the heart's slow, driftwood drying?

Does the body, uprooted,
die at an airport search?
Or is that just the death
of what we loosely call the spirit,
voice burning through the walless bone?

That Year

When rain came through the roof,
a sonata of wings released into my life,
I longed for the quiet of joy—something akin
to the body turning in dream's incalculable space.
I did not write poems about landscapes. I wrote
about grief's apples, stacking up
beneath rafters, year after year, until their weight
opened doors.

It was a year of few clothes, a year when questions
became coats, arms reaching, like branches,
toward pitiless November skies.
Amanda's three-year old asked me
to measure the distance between treetops and stars.

I went to work. I swam. I drove.
I taught a former prisoner who at one point in her life
washed walls, over and over, until
her image shone.
I passed my hands along walls, listening
for their shoals.
I recognized the cry of a bird—
carmine on snow, my heart, and recalled how an artist once told me
that he painted open doors whenever he fell in love.

What was this, against shoes left on banks without their soldiers?
Did one dare to love in times when people disappeared?
And then you came, an afterthought of fire tending frostbite,
warmth so unfamiliar that it hurt.

Leaving Harvard

That year, my mother did not leave
the house from grief, as she knitted
words and untold stories into the grains
of knotted sweaters. A bit of shadow,
a broken silence, a copper button. She looked
as lost as she must have been when
the German soldiers went through the refugee camps looking
for blonde-haired, blue-eyed children.
Or perhaps it was only the rumor
of their coming, but it was enough to make her stay
in the same apartment on President Street
for twenty years.
So she knitted the seasons
into her scarves, and the fibrillating reds
of leaves in autumn as they rushed across
the pavement with dry life. She knitted
the fluorescent stalks of winter trees,
the electric hum of emptiness, blue ice of thought.

All that year, I was not sure if she mourned
my grandmother's death, or my return from Boston by train:
two suitcases stacked above my head, black gloves
sliding down my wrists as the landscape expanded
on the window's surface in dendrites of rain. I didn't know
why I'd dropped out of Harvard, the roots of this knowing
so deep that I could not dig them up without
taking myself apart. Twenty-five years of preparation,
the weaving of invisible theorems, the hope
that I would one day live in a brownstone in Manhattan
with enough room to dance and no memories of wars.
Still, I was so accustomed to leaving—leaving,
the only imagined path of the future, although
none of us would say it, we did not really believe
in a future. Houses, marriages, and wills were
for those who never had to part with their children
in a foreign country, for the ones who knew that tomorrow
their village homes would still exist. And so, I left without
knowing why, to write my mother's poem, or mine,

not even sure to this day, which of us went to Harvard
on a full scholarship, which of us left, and which
of us came back. All I can know for certain is that
every time a woman's home is razed on another continent,
I can hear dust settling in my voice, and know the only
real poem is a song without a room, a heart without walls.

Your Laughter, Running

The day the evaluator came,
you took the podium, rose up
the way words do when tears
lie deeper than the heart of bone.
"Stop crying son," you read,
your laughter running
further than my life would ever take me
from myself.
Your poem was about the times your father
told you to stop, or he would really
"give you something to cry about."
How you laughed and laughed as tears
streamed down your face,
sorrow released from its epicenter—
a patient wing of moonlight loosed from sand.
I thank you for trying to better my job,
for feeling what I could not say,
that somehow we are all abandoned
waiting for someone who might never return,
our birth names different from those given,
our grandmothers—mothers, our mothers—children
lying in floods of rising grass,
beneath the drone of bombers.
"What kind of world is this," I ask
in which love means never coming home,
home means "no house,"
just an October maple of sky:
A fist of sparrows beneath the ribs,
there, where the heart should be.

Zhuravli

*"Be well, native land, throughout the night.
We will return, to this very place, across oceans,
across rivers."*

If I could dance to summon storms,
rather than the artificial tears on windows
that look out from warm homes without feeling—
eyes of those who can no longer cry,
I could read the languages of wind
etching rock, shale of music,
song of the cranes:

> Song of my parents, song of a return
> to earth.

When my father was five a fortune-teller,
for the price of two eggs
predicted he would travel very far, and he followed
the open hands of rivers to another continent.
He has always been returning.

Father, it seems the ten-mile, Saturday walk
from school to your village
continues still,
but the crops are phantom
stalks of moonlight, perhaps, mere
memories of sheaves.
It seems that my dreams are feathers
I try to follow into this life, but they drop
at the door of my body, and I cannot find you.
I have forgotten the word for love.

You Are

You speak at the level of bone; you are
political. You know the growing poem in a woman's

throat is not far from her silence, thick as it becomes
with rape in wartime, buried manuscripts, inner rain.

You are in the place where a woman is. Her shadow
fits your body, and her shadow-arm is yours. Whenever

she moves, you move— whenever she dreams you,
you exist. You are political, you read her body's

letters without claiming them, you know
there is no owning another's voice. There is no

speaking a foreign language unless you have loved
in that language, unless you have made it familiar

by accepting the one untranslatable word as a word
that will never be yours, but the grain around which

your life will grow. You are political, you hear
the voice of sand, the sand of forgotten languages.

Without exposing her pain, you recover a woman's history.
You stand inside her silence like slow music darkening.

Social Distancing

i.

I make a decision to wear a mask when leaving my home, because I am at risk, and my mother is dying. She has dementia and does not yet know this. How easy it is to create the Other:

ii.

All storms are necessary. Without them, we would not recognize our stories.

I had to tell her this six months ago, but she forgot. It is better this way. It is better to live a daily erasure than to have time etched onto your skin. Here, a cloud gets snagged on a thorn: "Do you remember the day," she asks.

iii.

"You have six months to live," the hospital staff told her, and I do not know how one can stand that finality—the feigned precision, the grief. As a child, she sustained a blitzkrieg in a farmer's basement. The town was called the village of the crown. How ironic. Yet at 87, she returns, in her mind, to the city of the swan, recalling how she could not attend school there, but ran along a riverbank while American soldiers threw their lassoes to the wind.

How easy to be caught. How difficult to let go.

iv.

Once, before an air raid, my mother stood in the window of a toy store, just wishing to reach for that doll. On another day, she played with children in a field, just before the shadows of planes overtook them and strafed hills to the right and left, as they lay, face-down, on earth.

Are stones necessary? Is silence a form of propaganda, of stone—hurled at the unfamiliar lake because it is unfathomable?

v.

I think about silence. How easy it is to create an Other—not even the amount of time it takes to pull on a mask. Just last Sunday, I wore mine to the Farmers' Market. A stranger saw me, pulled up his scarf and averted his face, as though I were the illness and the cause. It does not take much. Put a stone in a child's hand and tell him who the enemy is... Put silence in a child's vocabulary and see if he ever asks for anything again.

vi.

Who lives? Who dies? Who decides?

Asking is being alive. Hunger lives at the center of that lake—the innermost heart where the stone is lost—What would we dive in for, after all, if not for that one submerged life: Was it there that the three men drowned? They were on vacation, partying, and did not know how unforgiving that lake might be. Was it the golden fern I looked for in those woods? The fern that flowered only for those who saw?

vii.

And where was the good, after my mother boarded that train with my grandmother, as the soldier walked past them, threw their suitcase out? Could one believe in anything- after that? Yet my grandmother smoked and read, helped others escape. The school. The wounds. Anna painted a railroad tie that stretched across her hand.

Give a child an ideology, and it might masquerade as rainbow for a time, until she confronts its texture—stained, smiling glass. Then—how should she walk to the other side of the world, without breaking?

viii.

The man who turns away in the aisle—it is the look that startles. How quickly I am made foreign. Did I ever talk to those three men before they drowned? Did I pass them unknowingly, during a summer's walk? Who found the books in the church cupola where my father hid them, fifty years after his village burned? Did a stranger write a dedication for someone he fell in love with—someone who died in resistance?

ix.

Once, I received a prayer mat in the mail, and used it.

How I loved you—those days in the Hudson Valley. How you thought of the universe as a swing, and how we found it one day, water flowing upward on Peace Road.

x.

These days, I take walks and photograph a bright green lawn. I believe the branches on the ground are my feelings, but I do not want to bend. Deer cross the road, one by one.

We are not in the present. We are not in the past. My grandmother's suitcase is trapped in mid-air, but the train moves on... After years, I visit a museum; the work is there—an image of her hand, the rails, the wood. It is wood we carry within.

xi.

My father never saw his father again. Today, they meet in a field where there are no bombs, and his father says, "Go now, I have other children to protect." In my dream, my father's youthful lover was deported, but returns.

I rowed in that same, weathered boat. Somewhere, the sky breathes.

Three children escape. Later, three daughters die—of silence. My grandmother smokes. Circles waft on air.

xii.

Passaic gets its first ice-skating rink. No one owns skates, yet donations arrive.

No one drowns.

Chance

  Light passes through you as it suffuses a blade of grass, flickers on your surface, and makes you insubstantial. Your mother is dead. You are space made visible: water cupped by a hand, the wind's river in the marshes, or an arched back practicing

 its language of motion. You ask me if it could happen to you. What can I say?

  You can cut steel on the world's edge. My father, a refugee in World War II, escaped being shot because his intuition told him to choose a road instead of the forest. Chance is neither intuition nor fate, but the place at which those invisible lines intersect. The night is a gourd and we are its seeds, scattered at random and without care.

  What can I say as I see you whiz down the hill on your bike, eluding worry

with your reckless speed and flicking stars off your coat? "Look— no hands," you cry, before you stretch them out into the darkness.

A Daughter's Song

"Nightmare begins responsibility."
—Michael Harper

Nothing in my life prepares me for this:
In a room as large as a basement,
they work, bent over checks,
as though there would never be any place left
to see. When I walk through the door, her friends
cheer wildly, "Here comes Maria's daughter!"
Not since my graduation have I felt
so oddly like a pop Madonna,
warmly venerated, welcomed, loved.
Honey-dark light flows
near staggered boxes at their feet.
Young women blast radios; men argue
in different tongues, leave their tables
no more than twice a day.
My mother, over sixty, with phlebitis, pushes
a heavy box of checks aside. The work will be finished
later, sheaf after sheaf, coded by hand, while cartons
are filled and quickly removed, repeating
the rhythm of a railroad if it could
run over the tracks inside your body,
keeping time.

How I would like to see my mother cry
on the hour-long drive home,
but she stopped crying years ago, even learned
to help the others on her team by coding
faster than anyone, moving her pen
over stems of numbers, thinking of nothing
but finishing by five.
I would like to know how, at home,
she stands reading Joyce, Rhys, and Stein
for the first time in her life
and loving them,
saying, "This sure beats magazines,"

or "Do you have another book
like the Garcia Marquez I just read?"

I would give her another life
if I could, one that did not suffer
the skywriting of beauty,
abuses, the assurance of outstanding jobs,
coveted possessions, jewelry, summers
in the Catskills, expensive lessons
in designing clothes.

"If I only had an education," she confides.
"If only I could have gone to high school,"
and I ask myself how much
a person needs to prepare in order
to enter a room wide as false hope,
to believe that this is not a test,
that somewhere the parameters of language
become real, as that black rose of shadow
we call grief.

There Should Be

There must be those among whom we can sit down and weep, and still be counted as warriors. (I make up this strange, angry packet for you, threaded with love.) I think you thought there was no such place for you, and perhaps there was none then, and perhaps there is none now; but we will have to make it, we who want an end to suffering, who want to change the laws of history, if we are not to give ourselves away.

–Adrienne Rich

There should be a room in the deepest heart of the day,
in which we can rest, where webs of autumn shadow dissipate
against the shock of unexpected warmth: words of a stranger,
voice of a color, flame of a dance.

And yet, the heart grows tired, and the hands grow tired
by the weight of things we cannot carry, tired
by the ticking, the vital pulse of seeds
trapped forever under concrete fields—

as we are, the single parents or the adjuncts among
us, starting winter cars, slowly heating our windshields
for essential clarity of vision, as spare winter forests shed
their leaves, and thin lines of water become trees.

Tell me where this room is— not escape, but a meeting
of one survivor and another, the walking into a vein
of shadow, walking into the color of voice,
the leaning into a waiting body that has listened

for years with the hunger of its patience. Tell me
where it is I can watch the news of Robert Champion
without closing my eyes, and still see. I am looking
for that room, perhaps the place where warriors go
to weep is one where there are neither warriors nor victims,
a room where words have no walls. If here, or elsewhere
a woman calls for her missing son, then her song rises
in my bones like morning between the rafters of space.

Accident

You startle me with your brilliance, you speak
in poems not because you want to, but because your
memory fails. Near an abandoned prison, deer,
fenced off, run in herds for generations,
blood banging with the redolent wildness of grief.
You read Thoreau and Dickinson,
Sartre and Rich, each page rendering the one
before it blank. Yet words about healing imprint themselves
beneath your skin—bare bones
of leaves, pale phosphorescent stems.

Tell me how it is I can help you, angry bang
of entropic wisdom, beeper in your pocket, hungry for joy.
Who will rescue your anger from riptides of loss?
Who will match your sandy phrases with eroded recollection?
Who will run with you head-on because youth does not walk, no matter
how far there is to go?
Listen to me:
The world is full of hunters.
Be careful, still, rise
in your lived strength,
in the way you give birth to yourself daily,
in the way you wait and wait until all thorns fall
from your voice.

How do they know what it is to wait until
names sift down through your hands, a few grains of light
on the ocean's bed? What are grades in the face of hunger? What
are words in the face of survival, of trust? Not
the utterings of connoisseurs,
but what we use to summon
our lost children, or the bread we feed to shadows
that come home from war.

I tell you:
take your time until the world slows down,
until intelligence is measured by a love of the sea,

until a dissident is not a ruler's hunted twin.
Take your time, observe a cloud's slow breathing,
read rivers on a woman's aged face.
Offer water, be careful.
Do not swallow stones.
Then teach me how to write
as though there were only
five arrows left.

Other

You wanted to be me, but could you listen to silent water changing direction beneath a woman's skin? Could you hear dark glass breaking at the center of your lover's dream? Could you feel the earth chattering with life and roots and rumors of stone beneath your feet? Could you understand what students did not say to you—how some of them were beaten, how others went to war and left their knowledge in another country, looked at the world as though there were nothing left to learn? And did you swallow the wind when you cried? Did you wake up in the middle of the night like a storm tree shaking off beads of rain, the terror of healing so real that you could no longer taste it? And did you hear the wide silence in a refugee's dark eyes? And did you write as though there were nothing left to publish, as though there were nothing left to leave behind?

The last time I saw you, you raised your glass at a reception, and a wedge of light curled against its transparent skin. It was as though you held a hemisphere between your fingers, where faces stretched out toward the rim in exaggerated grins. From where I stood outside—a woman, a refugee, a flood—I envied you, professor. Your shirt smelled of beaches. Your world was so safe. So agreeable.

lena speaks:

one day I fail an exam and no one knows why no one knows the phone calls I've been getting and the looks and the walks to my car and the lectures on why I'd rather talk theory than roses and no one knows why I don't have a heart for these things why I don't have a mouth for them either no one no one knows why I drop out of school and lose years to dull work and quarrel with male shrinks who suggest that I always want to be on top no one no one picks me up when I fall when I crawl on the ground and my life writhes under silence like a snake of false words no one listens to my silence to a tree that grows behind my back year after year soon its apples are beyond my reach and its shadows become my spine no one listens to my gestures speak to the way I cry behind your back like a leaf turning in a windless sky cry like the bone-white skin of a star twitching in space no one

so I have lived and I have done these things and more and I have carved my words out of the silence of my bone and I have dripped white rain of song and I have taken every word from the black earth of my thought and I have taken every word from my children never conceived and I have written down hope in braille and followed blindly its staccato path and I have lost everything once and then again and I have been proud and crescent thin—almost invisible

so tell me how I should theorize these things because I feel that those who theorized my academic decline did not think it would ever really happen if they did they would

have used different words used words I understood and I would not have failed have failed with a nearly perfect academic record so tell me how you theorize the sound of your life falling stillborn through your body and the way that you bend to pick it up

and the way that you bend and the way that you bend and the way that you rise because you simply choose to do so because you simply were that close to dying because you found there was a mortal cost to saying I read paul celan because I love his work I love it and no more no less than that

You Tell Me

It is difficult to laugh without the knowledge
that a bad day brings, that the lisp of light on water,
the insect, the rind of music on a beach are all

there is, all we are given—definition in the sands
of seconds, black and white, nothing more.
This is what it means to sing:

to measure time with the grain of your voice,
to go beyond time with the aberrant half-beat.
Somewhere in solitary a man sings against

his life, desire breaking the injunctions of silence,
blood becoming silence again, but the memory
of sound is deeper than his voice.

You tell me you have lost your voice, and you believe
that it is everything—it is not even words
but the roots of shadow anchoring real trees.

Van Gogh: Church at Auvers-sur-Oise

Blue of windowpanes that do not see,
blue of midnight waiting for the moon,
blue of time growing thicker in love,
blue of the deepest layer of water become sky,
blue around which temples are built,
silence around which lives are bent,
aster-blue of winter stars growing without sound,
blue of the roots of music before they flower,
blue of courage gathering like a storm,
blue of open irises, of thoughtful dresses,
blue of sapphires humming beneath ground level,
blue at the black edge of coal, at the rim of fire.

All of this you saw, because you sifted through moods
of color, lived the color as though it were your voice.
You who listened to the universe, who heard
the spaces between its bones of light, who painted
families, fruits of stars, secrets,
who heard winter rain inside your sleep
but did not become cold for the life always waking you—
who painted waiting selves we could not see,
who listened to light shifting in the oceans
of our quiet days—you knew the point
at which light breaks and becomes human.

Winter Morning, Montclair

(After George Inness)

A tree breaks the field in half, as though
memory, too violent for dream, falls into dawn.
The grass itself is peaceful: Wood shavings
scattered across a frozen surface;
here and there, reeds summon deep water,
in ways that lovers recall mistakes.
In this museum, time, like water, is distilled.
Elsewhere, children hug tanks.

I, too, can freeze, become the oak's striated skin.
I can stand here forever, transfixed.
But then—the figure of the grandmother, her back turned,
quietly sweeping light.

All she holds are branches, yet what she gathers
is ice. There has been
a near-hurricane in my county, and I imagine
a survivor on her porch, making quilts of days
against a sunken roof.
Hands move over the blood's quiet hum.

I want to ask the woman in the painting who she is.
Why, with shoulders stooped, does she refuse
to turn around? What is her sorrow, and how cold?
Does she know that in Haiti, a mother trapped
beneath concrete tells her husband she will love him,
always?

She will not talk to us.
The winters, the wars, the impossibly slow mornings.
What else, after all
is there to say?

Past the half-life

of grief, what remains is the self beyond whatever it can lose.
At home today, we hold each other, cry black stars of tears

as leaves of sky close around us so tightly, we forget
all of those still with us who are dead. Just for once, you become

the young man you were before Viet Nam, ride your bike
in a storm without bullets, the rain so beautiful, it breaks

like laughter.

Tattoos

He sees me from within, eyes of my music. Light scrapes the inside of my bones,

healing so harsh after years of dark, and it is he—dancing, transparent feather. I have felt so much.

Passaic, my father dying. I carry lead in my heart. Lead. The years peel behind our backs like paint, in silence. And yet we love, like rivers—riddled with bullets of dream.

We grow larger for the holes in our wishes, where single parents can rest. Larger for our parents' love, now buried beneath the day's long page.

Take a walk with me—I don't care where. I knew you because you listened. To everything I could not say—how words, beneath my eyes, pressed against the arc of my tears, how stars turned in my blood, how grief's paper-thin light cut my tongue.

Mythologies, for anyone who reads. Touch my arm and understand—this life, ripening for you. I wake and forget that I have cried, with only salt to deepen memory.

Take away the pastels and the green lawns, the "hellos," and suburbia. Take away the boredom and the easy life—the shoppers trying to be characters. I need the memory of stone, the stone of speech, Demosthenes' mortal syncopation.

At Home

After the long drive from New York,
I recall that evening in the hospital. Midnight—
my father curled up like a tendril,
a tight bud of veined confidence under the ribs.
He was a secret that would not unfold.
I summoned the story of the rabbit and the frog:
The rabbit, always afraid of its own shadow,
was heartened, upon first meeting,
to see the frog leap into a pond.

And so, I explained his upcoming surgery as merely
fear leaving fear in the same way that water
passes through water. It is true that fear
never really knows its source—echo, running away
from loss.
Moving through time, as through
underwater shadows,
I told stories, understanding
how words stretched out before me,
crescent minnows becoming
invisible
in depth.

If there were angels in the room, I did not hear them,
only the muffled swish of a broom removing dust.
Is this how one slowly forgot?
Moved backwards through tense, as over
a string of beads?
Turned off the TV?
Dream of snow within dream:
How will my grief become a shore?

X-Ray of a Winter Landscape

X-Ray of a Winter Landscape

I.

I'm afraid.
I had forgotten the body was this brittle.
A woman whom I can no longer recognize
and I,
hold out our hands to each other,
but it does no good. She laughed and swam,
laughed and swam, while I wait
for my X-ray, having been told
that I might be very ill, might
never recover, might just have to wait like this
for the rest of my life.

I wait.
She taunts me with her confidence.
I envy her long legs,
fearing that she might outrun me.
I don't want to go in.
Outside, we stand,
under a winter tree, with shawls
of shadow draped halfway
over our arms.
Each within herself. Alone.

The woman who I no longer am
knew how to get through the days.
Now I do more than survive.
I have to.

I write.
Or I would be numb. Today,
I am my mother running to a doll hospital
before an air raid to claim
what she can't have, fear for her life
making her want without fear.
Today, I don't care about small talk.
I wear black stockings and a sweater-dress,
walk as though there were everything
left to find.
There's an orchard of stars in my dark silence.
Not this cold, this barrenness,
this graphite spine of a December landscape.
I'm looking for something that escapes
irradiation, for words that fall
to my feet like fruits
obeying gravity because they must.
I'm looking for something, for life

beyond health, beyond incipient
perfection, something, something,
that keeps falling, an arc of light
that repeats the curve of a shoulder
that repeats the curve of a river,
that repeats the outer bank of hunger,
something that asks us to wake
for no reason, to move
for no reason, to dream
like moving water or deep rivers of wood.

II.
Poetry is DNA,
a tree of words inside my body
growing silently beneath my skin.
Yet today, I would break out of myself,
lose myself in a forest of crowds,
forget my own name.

III.
The women of Srebrenica
nameless in their grief,
have no time for poems.
Perhaps this is not true.
Tonight I see a woman
praying with her hands,
folding dough into her apron
for her disappeared son.

Each night, she puts a braided loaf
on her sill. Each night,
each night, she never sleeps.
Black birds come to her house,
and mark the hours with their greed,
yet blue grains of sky
sift through her fingers,
each morning, each morning,
rivers of song.

IV.
And then you came to me, one night
like someone I had lost in childhood,
black hair like a river,
eyes too deep for wading.
We knew too much, too much
so you sang to me, not father,
not brother, not son, you sang
and touched my face until dark birds
were driven from my voice.

V.
I lie on a flat steel table
while cold metallic branches
move over my head.
I think about my days in publishing
about how editing X-rays language.
Does it make anything better
this branding of syntactic laws
onto a winter landscape of words?
Turn right, turn left.
Allow no broken letters
to enter the text.
Don't look into the X-ray machine
and its huge, clapping shutters.
Avoid the center of things.

Get on the subway and look at the floor.
Drink liquid. Don't taste.
Walk, sit. Stand, sit.
Eat, don't savor, or you will want
real food and be unable to get
through the days.

I want whatever is uncensored,
a language of broken letters:
I do not *really* want these things
but the fissures of their truths
that run like fault lines
through our camera lenses, bodies,
continents, our ashen waters.
I'm afraid. I wait. I write.

Matryoshka

The outer woman dresses well, with impermeable patterns and bold red prints. Enamel flowers are all she can offer, created as she is by other hands. This is a poem about the way things go unnoticed, about the way you are taught to dress well against all of life's daily questions, not a thread hanging frightened from your hem. A poem about

the way you memorize long lists of words, year after year, a kind of beaded amulet against the draft of other languages and their hints of prisons and spells. This is a poem about the precision of your speech, the affected pronunciations of an English grammar afraid of its own body, a wooden tongue afraid of its own roots.

The next woman listens. She can hear seconds tick in quiet bones; can grow a huge belly full of the world's complaints. It is a commonplace that women were born to listen, and they do. But who hears the riffs of rain blowing through their bodies? Who hears the silence, the sadness, the thorns? This is a poem about putting your grainy nature aside, opening yourself up until the many parts of you are scattered

on the table because it is the only way you know to share your innermost self.

And you cannot even get to the outer woman from the innermost one, because they have not painted hands on your body.

The next woman is closer to the center, and you will notice, in the world's eyes,

she is smaller. The woman within the woman within the woman does begin to write

and sing and talk a great deal more than before, but this disturbs the outer shell. The outer woman is thin and easily broken. This is why men like to hold her. Yet the woman within the woman within the woman has been trapped so long she has a great deal to say. She is a nuisance at board meetings. She is not sporting designer poppies. If you stand closer, you will notice that she is not small; she has been stooping all her life in order to accommodate this idea of largeness. *She is not small.*

   The woman at the center is wise and unpainted, difficult to grasp. Yet she rattles

in all of the others like a thorn, so that no one in the city can sleep. She has no clothes.

No one will hire her, though they take her apart to see what she is made of. Though she tries to warn the others, they do not understand her language. Sometimes she is thrown out for her vigilance. So she finds herself young or naked or homeless or crazy, a saint,

a witch, a poet on the subway, a root without a tongue.

Thinking

It would be like kneading dough, except that you would knead in the sky

and the atoms of shadow that collect in trees. You would knead in the cry of a man

about to leave his country, the stars that turn within his body and lead him out

of the forest at night. You would fold in fruits of darkness and rinds of sunlight.

You would remember hunger, black holes for weight. You would add in bits

of the morning paper for leavening. You would watch light bend at your table.

You would watch your lover's arm repeat the motion of light. You would think.

You would love. You would braid the rivers of the earth.

A Practical Poetics

i.
Poem:

roots too deep
for drought, for bleach
of sun, accolades, po-biz,
sabbaticals,
praise, those roots
too deep
for hunger.

the poem
pulls you toward yourself
like the swift undertow
of dream
or love waiting
in another country.

the poem is material, dark
as a lover's body, palpable
as its lack, the poem
is phantom pain.

the poem suffers
like a child, but laughs—
a sage
who knows that time
never cries.

in case you believe
the poem is soft, it is
the heart's negative space:
the heart resides in the body
but the poem embraces
the pulse, the blood, the rivers of the world.

ii.
Rivers:

a friend, lying on the grass near the susquehanna, looks up to
the trees and says,
"that space in the branches there is a broken frame. look! It's
you climbing out of your life; it's you climbing out of box after
box after box." what if i lose the innermost box,
i wonder. "you can carry your past and your sadness, as long as
it doesn't contain you."
words explode frames.

be careful. words also frame. just the other day,
i read that gossip is a form of moral policing: he did/she did/she
is is is. we are all guilty of homestead morality before the
wilderness of questions. careless psychiatry is log-cabin gossip,
demarcating boundaries plank by plank. an intern works with a
group of doctors who won't treat a woman without a home,
because she is mentally ill. propriety is the ruler that comes
down on her hand. what are the markers of judgment? does it
take one sixteenth of an inch to slide too far toward freedom,
toward the unmarked field? what are the diagnoses? the
medicated can't question. an entire country saved by Prozac
never asks "from what?"

poets ask. lovers ask. only the dead don't ask.

so tell me that this poetic endeavor is just a matter of posturing,
and then tell me why they kill poets in hard times—not for the
high salary, surely, not from greed. poets talk back, hurl their
vertebrae of words, break their own bodies to find them. so tell
me why the silenced die. all of those experiments with prisoners
in solitary and children never spoken to. words are life. words
are both unsettled and sane. they lead us out of ourselves and
corral us. so take care. be free. be careful. watch those diagnostic
acronyms. take finely-crafted nothings with a grain of salt, and
remember that unexplored rivers are not the real thing.

In the Camp

A woman, a bone
made brittle
by dreams so radioactive,
that their half-lives
turn to cloud,
walks toward a truck.
Beneath the tarp, among planks
she finds the crescent belly
of a fish exposed.
She reaches over, steals the fish—
a young girl eloping without thought.
It is an act of love, as is
the presence of hunger,
or the sound of water crying as it winds
through the heart, intuiting life.
Her eyes turn toward the wind's
open door, she slips
the fish into her pocket,
runs past barbed wire that snags
long sheets of artificial light.
When she reaches the barracks,
the scales
have frozen to her body
and there are fifteen years left
in this place.

What Words?

In a club, some men approach
my childhood friend,
ask her,
where she's from, as though her accent
makes her foreign.
They do not know the names
of rivers in her parents' homeland,
of thistles
that will not grow here,
of tea leaves that take on the light
color of grief.

I want to ask them
if they ever dreamed in a language
they could not understand—
discovered love caught on the other side
of slow translation, questioned
what it took
to name a new country before words.

And what words did they find
for the red moon rising in Passaic:
caesura in a poem of steel?
There are words
for languages buried with people,
names lost with children.
These words, these names,
are what we defend with our
shifting shadows— syllables
resisting northern light.

Dream's Long River

If you want to know if there is love after war, ask the sea.
The sea has no grammar.
The sea is breath.
The sea
does not judge.

Cast a stone beneath its surface.
Think of water as your love.
You will need to swim into that starless quiet
far beneath waves and their skin
where birth and death embrace.

What is right or wrong?
Ask the sea.
Ask dark, silent rivers of sky.

Look for the difference between shards
and green glass,
survival and song.

—————————————————————

Як хочеш знати чи лишається
любов по війні
запитайся моря.
Море не знає граматики.
Море є віддих.
Море не судить.

Кинь камінь під воду.
Обійми глибину як любов.
Треба плавати в тишині без зір,
далеко поза тіло хвилей,
де уродження овіймає смерть.

Що є правильне або зле?
Запитайся моря.
Запитайся темних, тихих рік неба.

Шукай за різницею між розбиттим знанням
І зєленим шклом –
пєрєживанням і життям.

The Violence of Things Unnoticed

At the edge of the ocean, a gull,
cry flung from the deepest night of bone:
It might be the song of a woman
walking home at midnight,
the hyperbolic curve
of hunger running
toward and away from life.
It might be hunger itself—
absence, or desire.
It might be the woman I saw on Fifth Avenue
thin leaf, shaking
for lack of home.

Fractals of Rain

i.
The horses, both facing the hills,
stood so close to one another
that they might have been hatred and love.
I have been tired, sleepless, past the fires of this city,
past green, broken ribs of poems,
past rumors of shootings,
the Galapagos Night Club,
ferns of smoke that become the spine,
leaving ash in the mouth if you let them.

ii.
In Vermont now, I am
from "somewhere else," even in my hometown,
"foreign." My language's patina suspect,
a deepening light, the self's aging wine.

> *What is the distance between freedom and a doorframe?*
> *Star and wood? A person in recovery I knew,*
> *tried to comfort her mother before she died, landed*
> *in the hospital from grief—*
> *worked at a woman's prison.*
> *A woman's prison is where you go as enforcer of rules,*
> *if you have broken all of them and have no other place to live.*

iii.
At the end of the college block,
just before the war begins,
a young man holds a woman
against the backdrop of a widening street;
standing there, they are fractals
against loosed sheaves of rain blown here and there by wind.
I think of someone I loved,
no longer with me,
fall back, in that moment between
bars of remembering and open spaces
where the horses stand, oblivious of everything,
leaves of night enfolded by leaves:
Rodin's body of a sculpture still asleep
inside the memory of stone.

The Sky Inside Your Body

I Walked

To get to the library, I passed
elegant *bodegas* and churches, men scarred
by imagining:

I saw
keys without children,
de Chiricho shadows, more palpable than doors.
The neighborhood gathered one day. "Don't look," my
grandmother said:
A man had hurled his mother from a fifth-floor window.
I passed magnolia-roots breaking through concrete, their petals,
scrim of life.
I passed marriages written in hopscotch,
the Capitol Theatre.

I kept
the feather that drifted from my pillow,
the day thieves tore our house apart.
I walked.
with my best friend in school
when she got pregnant:
Five miles to the library, the space between
a life and its book, if you were lucky to find
the right question.

Heels
worn
down
marked
time.
Stories fell from our bodies, one by one—
pages of earth let go by constellations.

Jackie married early. Camila stopped painting.
I remembered
outlets opening their doors and gathering
my teachers.
I carried home books that grew heavier

with distance as Billy Joel sang "Piano Man."
I carried
the knot inside of my mother's wish
that never became a life.
Additions were phantom pain; for every problem solved,
another death, yet, love without dimensions grew
larger than hunger.
(An artist fell off the scaffolding).

I loved
dance halls, the butterfly effect of tangos,
ripples of song in the blood giving voice
to grief's drowned stone. Cheap portraits
replaced fish, torn shades of industrial sunsets
held down with string, prayers over food,
the chaos theory of beauty deciding
who remained:
One constant was the lottery:
There were
no kites for children.

Freshman Composition

Is it because I taught you that it was all right
to cry, that you did—
that you wept openly at my crutches,
tears drumming on your cool black leather
jacket—rain loosed from a ground beat of slang,
hail of gritty *wannas* and prayers?
You were not like the men I knew,
who from habit, cigarettes, or cries
dropped only in soft, smoky feathers of song,
circled downward
with years,
so slowly that they disappeared
without note, their unspoken psalms engraved
on childhood swings inside their bodies,
listening church pews.

This is for you, and for all of the men
I knew before you who never asked me to dance.
How I hated them: how my grades, my poems
set me apart,
how I never planned a town-hall wedding soon enough
to pay my bills. How night after night I heard
them beat their sons' soft backs,
how their daughters left them,
how they cried without knowing
what they had ever done.
Perhaps it was the textile foremen
who knew nothing about sky,
or the hours of standing,
or the broken syntax of postures,
or the vodka, the riptides of music,
the longing to go home to wheat fields
pared from their shadows in the arid light of bombs.

Did they sift through basement tiles
of recollection, visit black and white stills
of schoolgirls abandoned
on their grandfathers' shelves? Did they waltz

with unborn lovers in ways they could never
dance with their wives? It was as though
a momentary leaning toward the reddest heart,
a wound of touch, the evening rose
of darkness closing inside a cathedral of palms
was enough to summon all the feeling on this earth.

Untitled

On the field beyond my porch, deer gather
like sparrows of silence at the edges of guilt.
One leaves the herd, flies, like a promise briefly
remembered.
After the hedges shift, blue quiet settles in again.
It has been a long time since the deepest self
became a poem, lover, a familiar street. Ages, it seems
since we met, hands moving over braille of bodies,
reading what we could not speak, that you, a medic,
and I—broken—
could somehow drink deep water again.
How, when the world exploded around us?
When border deserts ran dry, women walked in heels
for work?
You carried me, as over
the river of my life.
"In case I had to," you said, and I wished
you could let go of Viet Nam.
I wished that we,
could fall through the rifts in our lives,
like tears, in this moment balanced,
between today and today,
this hush of deer,
waiting for rain.

In Search of Stories

All of you who do not read poems
who do not hear the seeds of *salsa* ripening
beneath the asphalt of a winter street,
who do not notice desire asleep on the train,
who do not want change, do not want love,
all who trade a good cry for slick,
analytic talk of sadness,
all who know only the game,
the artifice of art,
who take
lessons in dancing without knowing how to bend,
who never look into a long day's open eye,
who believe war is a theater,
vulnerability a war, who do not care
if women are stolen,
who live too far from the black trees
of letters in your own hearts
to read them—as a result, you hunt deer
in search of stories.

Let Me Be You

It is what you hold back that tells me you are, *not as*	*Can you remember* who *a time when things were*
the way you shrug off feelings: *walk to where you*	*easy? Can you*
beads of water gliding off a leaf. *meet me at your kitchen*	*grew up,*
Listen: This is not a good way to live—	
always moving.	
	table where I now eat,
	hungry for words?
As though your pain would follow. *pick the long stem*	*Can you*
As though your solitude *industrial sunset, tell me*	*of an*
were a stretch of landscape *always feel alone?*	*why we will*
in your body: swoop of a phone wire, *change—*	*Some things never*
moonlit concrete, *the porch waits*	*outside,*

thorn of a fence.   *for the*
wordless laughter

Let me be you, love   *of fireflies,*
and I want to know

facing yourself,   *what the distance*
is

mirror against a dark sky—   *between a*
star and grasses of fire

distance, the last hand of cloud   *in Passaic,*
between a myth

vanishing.   *and a*
question, love

        and childhood.

    Let me be you, your hunger, myself.

I Could Have Told You

I could have told you that it should
not be this hard, that everything our parents
warned us about did not stretch
from the continent of one dream to the next.

Perhaps we should not have put so much
aside, the fear of loss so great
that we shored up moments
as though they were stones.

Perhaps we should have lingered
just a little longer at the place
where birches, suffused with watery
green light, settled quietly into dusk
at the river's edge.

The stories we heard, of relatives beaten
into the dark wine of silence,
of icons left in places
where no one would
ever pray to them again,
were enough to make us think
that time remained only for those
who did not know how to count.

Still, we lingered,
played bad records on our porches,
made trips to the Catskills,
stood unafraid while wind
blew in our faces, and caravans
of planets moved behind our backs.

We had to stop thinking, we had to live,
just live, feel the way that thin leaves do
as they lean into this thick rain of stars.

Ask Yourself

This is all I have, a poem,   *If you want to get to know*

spokes of pine turning in sunlight   *how a woman in*
another country

cirrus spines of sky   *braids bread, or*
how bodies of sand

leaves of shadow falling—   *blow away in war,*
you need to leave

people I knew, those who almost   *your hotel. You*
need to stand

made it. This is all I have: a page   *in the middle of an*
open square,

of earth, a tree, sky, body, names   *watch pigeons*
huddle under

carved on bark, dunes of jazz,   *a bench, hear shops*
stop breathing

wood, grasses,   *in the dark. Ask yourself*
what

syncopated consonance of love,   *you came for, if*
you would

words shaking off the rain   *live with a local*
woman, learn

of music until only sinews   *the words for*
cobblestones and fear,

of rhythm are left, until words *watch the flower of a*
winter sky

are bone-dark flint striking stone. *break into snow,*
ask yourself

This is all *if you would try to*
pronounce

I am—everything pared down *her name, at least that*
much,

to words, a woman saying *eat berries,*

"This is all I have. No more, no less." *syllables, her life.*

Ulster Heights, New York

As children, we looked out of our windows
when the aged reverend and his wife set out,
every evening to row. From our perspective,
they were spirits of trees,
etiolation of grief against a negative of sky.
The street had no lights, and we heard
their footsteps long after they passed: It was as though
everything they loved and sought to feed
hungered without name.
We imagined their lives before this summer:
A famine survived,
memories like herbs that did not grow here,
suitcases left on banks,
lost letters— fireflies rising.
No one understood,
why they pulled more fish out of that lake
than anyone.
Other seasoned fishermen imagined moonlight
carving circles on still water—
scrimshaw of history against
silence,
or silence—
obverse of song's rising bread.
Somehow, the lake yielded up its secrets
catch after catch.
But we knew it was the heart they listened for,
glittering with relentless scales,
unforgiving, fiery, and brutal,
as the war they fled,
night after night,
in sleep.
In truth,
it was love they plumbed—
nothing less than a net slipping soundlessly
over
a boat's mottled side, returning,
again and again
with forgotten life.

Bucha

The doors are gone
beneath a cloud's turning script.
Enter the children, stones,
giving voice to streams.
Enter the woman caught between arrival
and arrival.

To be trapped between the body and infinity—
breath and sky.
What is a life without doors?
Just a notion dividing
yesterday and yesterday—
This and that.
A quiet leaving, heard by no one.
A rape.
A face turned to the wall.

Who will wear her shadow?
Who will free her voice,
caught as it is, a bird in the throat?
In war, what is worse—
The blinding memory of love or burial,
death or its absence,
blood or light?

Elsewhere

I come for the deer—
this season, they kick up snow
in circles,
summoning clouds,
an ancient path of constellations
in the blood.

"Let your body remember," my Tai Chi
instructor reminds me, as scars
are a calligraphy of absence.

It is all in the breath:
Geography of skin.
What we know is on the other
side of bone.

Here, the pandemic creates silence,
prolongs the wait. I am
hurried out of the hospital, and still
am happy for the twenty something,
who forgot to go to work, then arrived
after too much wine.

The nurses keep
laughing, but his friend comes to take
him home.
No one would do this for them,
as they
miss the secret—
undercurrent, stone.

Elsewhere in cages children go quietly to sleep,
without any knowledge of the depth
that being held up by a river brings.

Today, the deer summon a storm.
They thunder through the woods,
white water,
just listening.

Winter Coat

Leaving the migrant camp,
a mother takes her daughter by the hand.
They walk along the path toward school.
A warm sleeve of wind envelops her,
until cold weather comes.
First the pain.
Then the numbness.
Then the education.
Walking past the distant hills, she feels
bread in the heart,
hunger in the heart of bread—
counts deer tracks, sees
galaxies of deer circling mountains,
life scaling stone.

With Doors Wide Open

Gravity

I feel that language should never be an escape. It is what you need to dig out of the rubble of your body. It is the earth of your body bearing witness to devastation; it is all you have when others come to ask, "What is happening here?" It is not a matter of posturing, not a matter of simply shifting a few polite stones, no—every time you pull up the earth you pull up roots, gravity gathering dust, the memory of water, dirt. This is the way it is. Then again, I have never witnessed a bombing which children called the Christmas tree, because there were so many lights that roofs were blown off houses, and so much ruin that villages burned down to their very roots.

Clay Birds

Toward the right end of the yard, the roof of a garage holds up a stretch of turf, and if you look past the fence, the staccato light of an afternoon sun bounces off hubcaps, wires, and some dishes that have been left collecting water for years.

I think we are all like that, waiting. I think we know there are things we can achieve, though we don't have the words for them, yet. I think we know that we stand in concentric circles of gardens: the gardens within our bodies merely intuiting light, our bodies, gardens, knowing where the skin's thorns begin, our bodies standing in that garden of at least a hundred roses—that garden, another circle within the greater circle of Passaic. I think we know where the skin's thorns begin, where women pray and yell at their husbands, when they are defeated and when they are strong, when they fold dough in church, create thousands of pierogi like clay birds that wake and fly toward warmer climates. How many secrets do they knead into that dough, how many hopes?

Renaming

What is love but language renewed daily? It is not the act of renaming, but rather, finding the hidden name in someone else, coaxing it out of them. What is language but belief, branches of sentences tending toward no conclusion, a single leaf turning in the windless sky? Renaming is an act of violence; people renamed are pried from their histories—unable to look in the mirror of the past, they do not recognize their beauty, but always look for affirmation elsewhere. This is a tragedy.

It happens to many women who "take one day at a time" because they have been convinced that no future exists for them.

Cobalt

Sometimes the nuns ask us to paint deer on the windows for the holidays—not stenciled deer, but real ones with wild antlers and knotted fur. At these times we are triumphant in a room full of empty rows without any prototypes for art. My friend's parents are school custodians—while they work, we work as well, tattooing animals on the night's skin, putting math problems on the board. I envy her ability to calculate,

to order—but most often I praise her magic: a few strokes of cobalt, and the sky looks like deep water into which stars sink.

It is at these times that we feel no authority above us, give mock lessons, sing our favorite songs. The hallways are empty of school patrols, and a river of evening silence washes over the tiles with a brisk December cold that wakes us up. "Whoosh, whoosh, whoosh…" Her parents wash the floors and we work on the glass with brushes and water, quietly sad at this reversal of things, wondering why it is that we are spared. Or perhaps we do not wonder, not yet having the words for relocation and war.

Perhaps we just feel the way a river feels with its inchoate language, moving forward without a thought. "Whoosh, whoosh…"

At School

At school we learn to chant in church Slavonic. We do this in the choir, Sunday after Sunday, following the deacon's premonitory, "hum, hum, HUM." There are no instruments, just the bare hands of voices scaling rock. I am happy when I sing. I can express my feelings in public. Most of the time, I feel I have to hide them, in the way that I hide my knees beneath the blue folds of my skirt, in the way that I never tell the nuns what I am thinking, just what I have learned. There is a world of difference between what we learn and what we think: What we learn is etched on the surface of our skin, and what we think is etched on the inside of bone.

Skylights

"Tell me, children. How was your day?" My friend's father takes our opinions seriously, and listens with exaggerated wonder to our riddles and questions. I am always gallant and self-consciously erudite, living up to the image of game-show scholars on TV. He does not know that I wonder where animals go during air raids, and whether my grandmother worries, waiting for me to come home. Every time I leave, she stands with the door open, thinks I may never return. "This room needs a door," my friend says. It is not coincidental that she includes skylights in each apartment. There are no air raids in her creations—only the flour of light pouring onto the page like a clear winter's snow.

I Don't Remember

I don't remember how it is that we come to understand one another, our various Englishes colliding in trust, our various Ukrainians playing tag. And I don't know how our friendship survives the divide between older and newer immigrants, speakers of dialects, and speakers of a 1950s version all competing for respect, for a worthiness sometimes denied them in factories, in universities, at home. We do not yet know struggle, though it rises over our shoulders, larger than life—the substance of life. We do not know self-hatred. We talk in the common space reserved for outsiders, the space off to the side of the school lot where the grass pushes up stones—so many syllables of grief.

Maps Carved on Stone

On Good Friday, the parishioners get on their knees and edge their way slowly toward the altar. Some are very old. Women wear scarves tied beneath their chins. Their faces are like arrested songs—some locked in sadness, others in joy. Watching them, I wonder what has brought them here. How many rivers have they crossed? How many degrees have they traded for jobs that have nothing to do with their fields? They kneel, because they know what the universe can do, yet it is not a gesture of fear, but one of deepest understanding. They know that they are stars at the tips of invisible grasses; they know that they can fall at any moment, so they sing.

Some wear mink coats, so as to bring their best to Mass. Some are painters. Some are plumbers. Some are teachers, nurses, doctors. Some are salesmen, workers, lovers, friends.

I wonder what has brought them here. How many clouds read in the hands of fortune tellers? How many maps carved on stone? How many paintings, candles—have they left behind in the night? How many children lost to war? They move in constellations toward the altar, brushing one another with their lives.

With Doors Wide Open

I have heard that in war-torn countries, people take brooms to their porches after bombing, sweep away bits of debris during that millisecond before the bombs fall again.

My mother knew the word for war. The language did not matter; once you had experienced devastation, you could never go to a tearjerker again. "Tragedy is for the young," she says, as a challenge to what many people think. Her youth was spent in D.P. camps in barracks, and she associates tragedy with youth, questioning the existence of horror films when so much terror resides in real life. "It is not an escape," she tells me. "One needs an escape." "You realize," she says, "that we left our home with the doors wide open."

Works Cited

Rich, Adrienne. *Collected Poems.* WW Norton & Company, 2016.

Harper, Michael. "Nightmare Begins Responsibility." *Songlines in Michaeltree: New and Collected Poems.* University of Illinois Press, 2000.

www.ingramcontent.com/pod-product-compliance
Lightning Source LLC
Chambersburg PA
CBHW020546080526
44583CB00013B/1022